The Farm

Memories of Life in Rural New York
written by the 9 siblings who lived it

Copyright © 2015
R. Perkins
All rights reserved.

ISBN: 978-1515181996
United States of America

Cover photos from top to bottom:
1. Ria and Lady
2. Ed, Paul, Matt, Becky, Ria
3. Matt and calf
4. Paul, Becky, Matt, Christa Ria, Ed playing croquet
5. Mom

Back cover photos:
1. Ed with the milk machine
2. The whole gang with Grandma and Grandpa Williams
3. Ria churning butter
4. Paul with Cleo and new barn
5. Susan at the "phone booth"
6. Lady (front) and Red (back)
7. Becky and Cleo in boat
8. Dad, Ed, Paul, Matt, Becky at well
9. Ed, Paul, Matt

Contents

Prologue

The Sobolewski Folly 1

Terry - Eggs, Rats & Snow 7

Susan – Manure, Snowmobile & Cigarettes 19

Ria - Milking, Reading & Sewing 33

Ed – Wood, Frogs & the Fish 43

Matt – Fishing, Work & the Pond 55

Christa – Demo Days, Decorating & Dad 61

Paul – Fun, Names, & the Barn 69

Mike – Wishing Well, Projects & Cold 81

Becky - Garden, Spiders & Walks 87

Epilogue 99

Prologue

This is a collection of stories from our childhood memories of growing up on "The Farm". It began with a story I wrote for a high school assignment called *The Sobolewski Folly*. Everyone loved the story and reminisced over it throughout the years. I cannot be sure who coined the name, but I'm guessing Mom or Mike. I certainly wasn't clever enough to come up with it.

Now we're all middle-aged parents, grandparents and retirees and our memories are fading (at least mine is!). When we share a story our perspectives are so different. Because we were all at different ages during our time on the farm, we have such varied perceptions of how it all played out. Since Mom especially loved the *Folly*, I wanted all of us to write some memories to share in this little book for a family keepsake. I hoped to have it ready for our mother's 85th birthday, and with a bit of prodding everyone came through! They wrote more than I ever dreamed. I expected a couple paragraphs from each, to form a small booklet, but the farm memories just kept coming.

The farm was such a big part of our lives, especially for the younger children, and shaped us into the people we became. If you are a stranger reading this, I hope you enjoy our stories. It was written primarily for family, but I thought I'd share it with the world and maybe someone would get a kick out of it. My parents were raised in the city of Utica, NY and did not know very much about farming when they embarked on this adventure. My father read *Organic Gardening* magazine, and probably anything else he could get his hands on for information, but those were days before Internet and you couldn't just look up anything at any time. Mistakes were made and some animals (chickens, mainly) died accidentally. It was part of the learning curve, and a story or two may disturb people who love animals, but we did our best and treated our animals humanely. They were grass-fed, happy cows, pigs and chickens. I encourage anyone who is dreaming of life on a small farm to figure out a way! Our father had a "regular" job so the farm wasn't our main source of income and that worked out well for us.

As we used to hear every week on Dragnet: THE STORY YOU ARE ABOUT TO HEAR IS TRUE. ONLY THE NAMES HAVE BEEN CHANGED TO PROTECT THE INNOCENT. But much of what follows is subjective, and there are no guarantees as to the accuracy. These are children's memories, recorded long after the events happened.

This book starts off with the original *Folly* story, then presents the other stories, written by each family member, in the order in which they were received. I edited only the tiniest bit for this book, allowing everyone's individual voice to come through, and I put my notes in [brackets]. I collected the stories from everyone so none of the siblings was influenced by the other's work, and I wrote my latest entry before I read the others' stories. Kudos to Terry for being the first one done!

Rebecca Sobolewski Perkins
July 30, 2015

Cast of characters & ages when we moved to the farm:
- Michael (Mike) 18
- Therese (Terry) 16
- Susan 13
- Christa 11
- Maria (Ria) 9
- Rebecca (Becky) 8
- Edward (Eddy) 7
- Matthew (Matt) 5
- Paul 3
- The Parents: Ed and Donna

Back: Mike, Susan, Terry, Grandpa, Grandma
Front: Paul, Becky, Eddy, Matt, Christa, Ria
Christmas 1973, 2nd year on The Farm

Mom and Dad, 25th Anniversary, 1978

THE FARM
Memories of Life in Rural New York

WRITTEN BY THE 9 SIBLINGS WHO LIVED IT

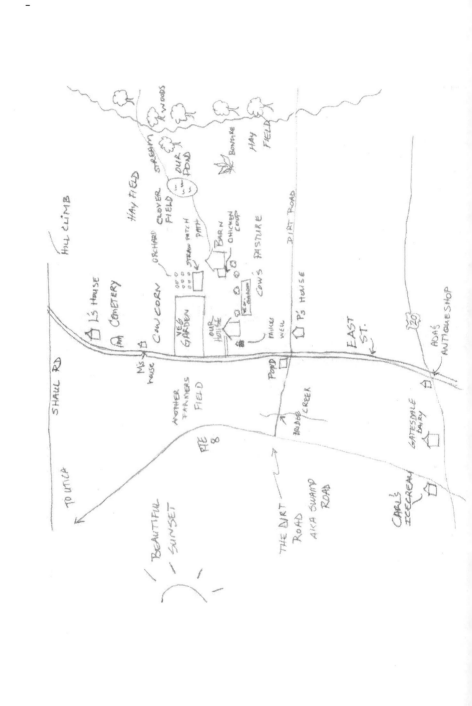

The Sobolewski Folly

the unedited original

by Becky Sobolewski, NY 1981

My story begins in 1972, the year we moved to our big old house in the country. We were a bunch of "city slickers" who had never seen a real cow, let alone drank real cow's milk. My parents had decided to move out of our 3-bedroom ranch house in the suburbs in central New York into the 6-bedroom house on East Street. It fit our family of 11 much better. When we first arrived at the old house, all of the kids' hearts sunk. The grass was over a foot tall and there was ancient machinery lying around in back. When we went inside, our hearts sunk even further. The place was a disaster area. There was furniture and junk everywhere. We were not moving in yet, thankfully. We were only there to start cleaning. The cleaning took weeks, partly because we were always stopping when we found some old pictures or junk, and partly because it was such a mess. When we finally did move in, the place was clean, but much work still needed to be done.

The barn was a fun place upstairs. It had a very high roof with a rope hanging in the middle, and all but the oldest kids swung on it. We had many good times in the barn, like haying a few years later. It was very hard work, but I always liked it because the family was together with neighbors helping. My father liked to talk about barn wedding receptions we would have, though none of the kids really liked the idea. The downstairs of the barn was a different story. The previous owner had left a herd of cows in the barn all winter long (or longer) and the floor of the entire barn was 3 feet deep with manure. The oldest boy, Mike, moved out soon after we moved in, so it was the job of the 5 girls to shovel out the barn. With the help of two shovels, a pick and a wheelbarrow we worked away at it little by little all fall. The previous owner had plowed a garden spot for us, so that is where we carted all of the manure, and spread it by hand. We got enough vegetables from that garden the first year to last all winter long, and have been getting enough every year since.

The next spring, 1973, we bought a little Ford tractor, so we could plow our own garden. It also aided in finishing the manure in the barn, which even with the tractor and manure spreader took the rest of the year. (The strength of 5 girls is limited. Our ages were 8, 10, 11, 13, 16 and we were only working on it during our spare time after school.) A lot of our time was also spent getting wood for the winter, and the barn clearing was low priority.

When the barn was emptied, it looked like a new place. You could even stand up straight in it without hitting your head. This is when Dad decided to buy a cow. The day the first cow arrived, none of us kids were very excited because we knew we would be doing the milking. I wasn't very pessimistic, since I was only in 4th grade and wouldn't start milking yet. When the cow got into the barn, my father, who thought he knew all about cows, squatted down and grabbed the nipple. Being a normal cow, she didn't like this sudden movement, and she kicked. I will never forget this episode as long as I live. That cow kicked right up my father's leg, and ripped a straight line up his pants. My father was quite surprised and pained, but not discouraged, and he asked Mr. P., who we bought her from, what he had done wrong. Mr. P., who had been standing there all this time, told my father he had to pet the cow and let her know you are there. When Dad did this, all went well. So went our first encounter with the dairy business. About this time, Terry, our oldest sister joined the Navy, leaving seven kids. One year later, Susan left.

Now my father began obtaining equipment for our dairy of one cow. We first bought a milking machine, since no one could milk by hand. Then we bought a hand crank separator to easily separate skim milk from cream. Next came the pasteurizer, cheese press and ice cream maker, plus another cow. You may think we couldn't use all that equipment for just 2 cows, but each cow gave 16-20 quarts a day. We ended up dumping a lot of milk out or giving it away. The solution? Pigs, of course!

We bought a couple of pigs to use up the excess milk. They were an interesting addition to the farm. We already had an electric fence to keep the cows in, but when my father put one around the pigpen, everyone got a "taste" of the electric current. While pouring mash over the fence in the pigs' trough, sometimes water or milk would drop on the fence, causing the electricity to run straight up through the metal pail and everyone had a chance to feel the fence. Even our dog Tracker learned to stay away from the fence after a few shocks. By now we were all farm kids, and loved to play nasty tricks on our "city slicker" cousins. We used to tell them that if they touched the fence with grass, they wouldn't get a shock. I think every kid who ever came to our house got a feel of that electric fence. I got so I would go way around it to avoid ducking under or jumping over, which I probably could have done with ease.

We bought chickens soon after the pigs. My father bought a bunch of chicks (about 50) and we raised them. When they started producing eggs, my father built them little nesting boxes and every week, someone was assigned to clean out the chicken coop – the most dreaded job on the farm. If you've ever been around chickens you'll know why. The smell is horrendous. Well, we stuck with the chickens for a year or so, and then we decided to use them for meat. We'd kill about ten chickens at a time. (Actually, my father did the killing with the help of my younger brothers. I stayed far away.) Then came the worst part—plucking. We gradually got out of the chicken business.

As we were building up the farm we were also fixing up the house. Everyone did their share of putting up wallpaper, painting, and adding their own personal touches to the bedrooms. We were also doing cleanup work outside. There was an old hop barn half fallen down, and my father hooked up our little Ford tractor and pulled and tugged at the barn. It gave a good fight, but finally it collapsed. We then had another problem: how to get rid of the pile. We sold a lot of the siding, but most of the wood was useless, and we loaded it on to an old manure wagon that came with the house. Then we dragged it up to a field where we had a huge bonfire. We took many loads of wood and burned many fires until that barn and any other junk wood were gone. We now had room to expand the garden and put in a strawberry patch.

The strawberry patch went in after three or four generations of cows, the house and yard in good shape, and everyone content with living on a farm. The three oldest kids, Michael, Terry and Susan moved away, and my younger brother and I had been old enough to milk for a couple years. The reason I mention the strawberry patch is because it was sort of a turning point on the farm. We were adding things for enjoyment rather than just survival. We also added an orchard at this time consisting of dwarf trees— apples, plum and pear.

We already had a thriving garden, which had supplied us with enough vegetables for all of the years we have been here. We had survived a blizzard in the end of May one year that had frozen the pumps in the cellar and we had to bail two feet of water out by hand. We had survived the backbreaking work of shoveling out the entire lower barn. We had survived the work of plowing, planting and harvesting a garden, the hot and tiresome work of baling and bringing in 200-300 bales of hay a year; and the work of cutting, stacking 10-15 cords of wood a year. The kids had survived being newcomers in school, and my father had survived two heart attacks, and was forced to retire at age 50. When my parents planted that strawberry patch of 100 plants, in 1978, we all looked forward to the luscious berries that were guaranteed to come two years later.

Well, the fruit did come in two years, and we got over a hundred quarts, but my father never got to see them. He died October 12, 1978 of a heart attack, the same year the patch was put in.

After that things seemed to turn chaotic. None of the boys could get along with each other. The next spring, 1979, a couple of kids, one being my brother, were playing with fire in the barn, and with all the hay it lit up like a torch. The firemen saved most of the lower half where all the equipment was, but the hay was gone and the barn was useless. We dragged everything out and my Uncle Tom Pelnik came with his bulldozer and plowed up the remainder of the barn. He dumped it in the same spot where we used to have bonfires years ago, and there it still sits. A new barn was built, but to us kids it could never match the old barn, that had given us years of fun. It had a very high roof with a rope hanging down the center, and we used to swing on it all the way across the barn and into the hay. The new barn has just enough room upstairs for hay and spiders – nothing else.

In the family all there are left are the three youngest boys, my mother and I. Everyone else has left and gone their separate ways, and soon we will be leaving this house for good. My mother and the boys will be going to Florida and I will be going to college in Boston.

Terry - Eggs, Rats & Snow

My first memory of the farm was actually the ride to go see it for the very first time. Dad took the dirt road. I have various explanations for this, but will let it go at that. I don't believe I was the only one weeping, or dreading what was to come. My heart sank when I saw the house. The lawn was well overgrown. The outbuildings were in varying stages of ruin.

What I found inside repulsed me. The kitchen and bathroom were disgusting, with sulfur water to boot. (Imagine brushing your teeth with hard-boiled eggs! I would make many trips to the well to pump water for brushing my teeth.) All I saw was filth on the main floor. When I walked into the room that would be our parents' bedroom, I slipped, went airborne, and landed on my back. Apparently, the dog(s) was allowed to do its duty in the house. This must have been its favorite spot. The floor was slimed with pee and doo. It's a wonder I didn't heave right then and there. I also remember the horsehair and lath [walls] in this room.

In other areas the wallpaper was peeling with layers of various patterns exposed. We left civilization for this?! I was sick with disbelief—that Dad thought this was a good idea, and that Mom went along with it, being a city girl and all. Total disbelief! Sainthood should be bestowed on her for this alone!

The best room in the house, in my opinion, was the one that would be mine. It didn't need any kind of work. It was bright and cheery. I liked the wallpaper, and the closet was a decent size. I do believe we stored potatoes in it! No heat, so it was really cold in the winter. A vivid memory I have occurred in this room. We didn't have screens on the windows, and mosquitoes weren't a problem because the barn swallows feasted on them. Anyway, I had a large tissue paper flower in one of the corners near the ceiling. I can't recall why I touched it, but when I did, a swarm of flies came at me. I flew out of the room and slammed the door. When I finally went back in, they were gone. Flies still creep me out today!

We made several trips there to clean up and make it 'livable' before we moved in. One of the first things Dad did was rip out the kitchen sink unit and toss it in the back yard. Hauling water from the well, heating it up, and doing dishes in a dishpan got old in no time, so he put it back in. We had a fine country kitchen when it was finally renovated.

The old stone foundation was crumbling in spots around the side doorsteps—one thing that was promptly corrected after the following incident. It must have been shortly after we moved in. One night Mike and I were watching TV, and I got up to get something in the kitchen. Then I saw a big rat sitting near the refrigerator. I quietly called to Mike, who got the broom, just trying to keep it confined to that room. The rat then turned and disappeared behind the fridge and out the hole he came in through. This creepy event happened before the flies.

The toilet was ripped out along with the kitchen sink. It was foul. The tub was nasty too. The bathroom was beautiful after it was redone. Looking back at it today, I don't know what Dad was thinking, because now it reminds me of something you might see in a brothel in Victorian days! [Velvety red wallpaper-see picture on back cover.]

Dad also put a toilet in a tiny space between the two back bedrooms upstairs, which was really needed. One bathroom was not enough. The upstairs was mostly heated with the wood stove, which was in the largest room. I remember sitting in front of it, stoking the fire, and Matt would brush my hair.

As if the house wasn't bad enough at first sight, the barn had its own horror, wall-to-wall layers of hay and manure. We spent months hacking away with picks and shovels. It was so high, I'm sure any cows that had the misfortune of being housed in there, had to duck their heads to walk from end to end. We were strong by the time this 'chore' was completed! And Ria would become pretty good at driving the tractor and hauling manure.

The hayloft was quite the contrast to the area below— massive space with lots of room, even with the hay that was in there. There was a big hole in the roof, which was soon repaired. I believe the Uncles came and helped with that. I remember after the manure was cleaned out and we had the pigs, we could go up in the loft and look down at all the little piglets when they were born. It was a good place to hang out for some peace and quiet, not that East Street was a hustling, bustling, happening place!

We all had our assigned chores, tending to the various animals. One day after school, I went out to milk Red, our only cow at the time, and when I tried to connect the machine, was promptly kicked across the room. The force of that kick tore my pants, wine colored wide wale corduroy, I recall, and really hurt my leg. It was the last time I milked any cow. After that, my chore was feeding the pigs, whom I called Blacky, Whitey, and Spot. Blacky was my favorite; he was the most friendly. The pigs were amusing. Dad used to stop at Tamer's Market in Whitesboro to get produce that wasn't suitable to sell—I remember lettuce leaves, oranges and grapefruit. The pigs went 'hog wild' over these treats. All three of those pigs ended up on the table!

I don't remember when we got the chickens, but they were the nastiest smelling creatures (their manure, specifically) on God's green Earth. Recently, I was at Mount Vernon, George Washington's home, and came upon a herd of sheep down by the river. I don't remember the breed, but they are the only animal that I've come across that rivals those chickens in their stench. Pig manure is sweet compared to their foulness. Home Depot sells Chickity-doo-doo manure, and if I catch a whiff, I wretch.

Dad used to keep an eye on the chickens to see who was or wasn't laying eggs. Those that he thought weren't doing the job, ended up in the hop barn, their fate being sealed. At least one was just a little slow in popping them out, and met an untimely demise. The evidence showed up in the postmortem...several stages of egg development were found. The pigs were the beneficiaries of these treats, and the doomed chickens eventually ended up in the pot. I was never around for the chicken plucking. I used to babysit Edie B.'s sister's kids, and those days conveniently coincided with the plucking. I do remember the smell of wet feathers, though... foul fowl. I worked in Old Forge during the first full summer on the farm, so I missed the haying season, as well.

Eventually we got another cow, Lady. She was sweet and docile. Red didn't take too kindly to her, and used to butt her. Red had horns. Lady did not. I'm not exactly sure when it was chronologically, but Lady had a stillborn calf. It was really heartbreaking watching her continually lick and nudge it, knowing her efforts were futile. We called on Alan P. for help. He took the calf up to the edge of the woods and buried it. Lady was depressed for a while. Red was dehorned soon after.

Mom and Dad were not at home when several events occurred involving the animals. One day the cows got bored with the field, found a way to get through the electric fence, and decided to go for a walk. We were all panicking, trying to figure out where they went. There was a huge field across the street, but they weren't there. The neighbors hadn't seen them. Eventually they were found somewhere down the dirt road. I don't remember how we got them back to the barn. (Mom may have been home for this one.) Another time the pigs got loose, and headed over to the cornfield. This may have been when I was home on leave, and Mom and Dad had gone to Old Forge for the weekend. Another fun day on the farm!

One day several of the kids were outside playing on the driveway side of the house. All of a sudden, there was a lot of screaming, so I went out to see what all the commotion was about. There was a garter snake on the side doorstep, and baby snakes off to the side of it. The snake was 2½ to 3 feet long, so I picked it up by the tail and hooked a crowbar under the neck, and carried it to the field. I saved the day! I've removed harmless snakes from several places over the years, so my husband refers to me as the "snake wrangler".

Living in the Snowbelt, we had a lot of snow. Many of my memories are snow related. The blizzard of '66 in Whitesboro, being stranded when flights were canceled due to storms, Christa going out in blizzard conditions to retrieve blankets from the clothesline, returning to New York from our honeymoon in the Bahamas. We were stuck in Syracuse

because of blizzard conditions. Mom hired a limo to bring us home the next day. Because of all the snow and drifting on East Street, it wasn't passable, so the driver ended up dropping us off at the Claradin Restaurant on Rte 20. Mr. B. eventually came and picked us up.

One time Susan and I were out snowmobiling along the fields behind the L.'s and the cemetery. The snow was really deep. We must have gotten off the track or were trailblazing, because we got stuck. The machines sank into the snow. I'm not sure how we got out of that one. We may have gotten help from Clifford L. or Michael, but I don't remember.

Speaking of the cemetery, I'm sure most of the family remembers that, particularly the Jabez headstone. It was a really old place with markers from the 17-1800's or earlier, and overgrown and surrounded by a thin line of trees.

It looked really creepy at night, especially when it was foggy. Whenever I came home from the L's after dark, I would run or peddle as fast as I could to get by it. You never knew who could be lurking behind those tombstones, waiting for someone to linger, and then pounce!

Debbie L. and I used to play cards or just hang out. One Friday night I was there, Susan may have been there as well, and one of our friends from school came by. Debbie had invited him earlier in the day. I'll call him "Bub". With some pre-planning, we told him that the cemetery was haunted and that we'd actually seen the ghost of Jabez. So we took a stroll down there to see if it would appear. After several minutes passed, a ghostly figure rose up from behind the Jabez tombstone. Bub was a smoker and, upon seeing this ghost, was halfway back to the L's before his cigarette hit the ground. Clifford had played the part perfectly. Wicked, I know. We had a good laugh about it after he left. I don't think we ever told him that the ghost wasn't real!

[The photo on the previous page was taken in 2004 when I (Becky) visited. The cemetery had been cleaned up recently, but during our time there, it was a jungle of periwinkle, wild pink roses and trees. The poem on the Jabez stone says *"Reflect dear friends as you pass by, as you are now so once was I, as I am now you soon will be, so prepare for death and follow me."* We understood it as a sinister verse, but as indicated by the Psalm inscribed on it, he was merely saying to prepare yourselves for death so that you will go to Heaven. He died Nov. 9, 1838, age 31 yrs, 4 months, 10 days. He was the son of Daniel and Cary Gallup. I can't remember what Psalm it was, but I did read it in 2004.]

Another snow story: One day in May '73 or '74, we had a snowstorm. Wet, heavy snow. We lost power and school was canceled for the day, but there was no sleeping in. Since we didn't have any electricity, the sump pump wouldn't run. To keep the cellar from flooding, we formed a bucket brigade to haul out the rising water. If I remember correctly, we started around 7:30 or 8 am, and went until 11 or so, when the power came back on. Then the sun came out and melted whatever snow stuck to the ground. A freak storm in May!

Funny, the things we remember. Like the Beetle. It had no heat. I remember lighting Sterno cans on the passenger's side of the car. So desperate for a little heat, we risked life and limb! One day—we may have been going to church—I went out and started the car. Dad freaked out. I didn't have my license, but I was 16 when we moved to the farm. I didn't see what the big deal was...

Some random memories: We had a party line phone service. If a neighbor was on the line, we would have to wait to use the phone...One day a couple of the sisters decided to cover Becky's head with fresh green burdock. It was quite comical. Matt had a language all his own which I think he shared with a stuffed animal. Yebba sabibba gizzie wingle! was one of the things he said. He was prone to tomfoolery according to one of his teachers. Ed thought he was Evel Knievel and tried some stunt jumping. It didn't work out so well. Michael used to shoot squirrels and dabbled in taxidermy. He also made up all the nicknames for everyone and tales related to them. His imitation of Susan walking in heels is classic.

We did a lot of walking and bike riding to get around. Susan and I went to West Winfield on several occasions. There was a great deli near the main intersection where I would go to get Italian subs. They made the best ones I've

 ever had. I used to go into the woods and up the hill behind the house. Raspberries grew wild up there. One time I went up there with Paul and Becky. We went on a really long hike. Up beyond the hill, we came upon a tree that was hollowed out. The trunk was large enough, so I had Paul get inside and climb to the opening at the top so I could take a picture. Then I had him stand in the bottom. I was laughing so hard at this sight that the picture was blurred. It's hilarious when the pictures are put together. I laugh every time I look at it. Paul was so cute and had a full head of "mole fur".

After we left the tree, we wandered through the woods, going further away from our property. Out in the middle of nowhere, there was a hidden pond. It was a perfect rectangle with dark green-blue water. It appeared to be very deep. I have no idea who owned it. We continued to walk, and finally ended up in a clearing on top of a hill. My memory is that St. Joseph's church was down below!

I have some memories of Tracker, such as Dad training

him in the kitchen, a piece of meat balancing on his nose. When Dad took him on a hunting trek, things didn't go as he had hoped. When he fired the gun, Tracker took off and headed for home. When Dad got back, the dog was cowering between Mom and the kitchen sink. Dad was ticked off, of course, and called Tracker a lousy, good for nothing dog.  He was no Missy. She was a rare dog. Tracker was no hunting dog, but was a great pet. After a time, I started calling him Beau (as in Beauregard). I may have gotten the name from something on TV.

Beau had another episode involving a gun. Not only did we live in snow country, it was also deer country. Dogs running deer was against the law of the land. They could be shot if they were seen in the act. Apparently, this is what happened to Beau. Or it could have been a case of wrong place, wrong time. I don't know how long he was missing, but when he finally limped

17

home, he had a gunshot wound. The vet said he barely escaped death. He made a full recovery. The last time I saw him was when I was home on leave in 1975. I had to be in Iceland on December 15th, so we had my Christmas early. He posed in front of the Christmas tree.

Although I only lived on East Street for two years, I have a host of memories. Only a few are mentioned above. Little snippets that easily come to mind. All of us learned great life lessons on that farm. Most people don't experience in a lifetime what we did in the years that we were there. Today a lot people believe our food comes from 'the store'. What a silly notion that is!

Susan — Manure, Snowmobile & Cigarettes

On "the farm", as we affectionately now call it, we had a hunting dog, Tracker (who was gun-shy) and several nameless outdoor cats for hunting mice, and an uninvited rat or two in the kitchen. We also had two milk cows, several pigs (and cute little pig*lets* who later became pigs), lots of chickens, a useless rooster that avoided the chickens and barely crowed. We had no goats, at least not while I lived there and we had only one sheep. It was black, and it was me. This is my story...or at least part of it!

It was the summer of 1972 when our family of 11 moved to the farm. The third oldest of 9 children, I was just turning 13. Having been raised in the suburbs, I wasn't exactly enthusiastic about the idea of moving out to "the sticks". The remote country town we'd never heard of was 30-plus miles from our little 3 bedroom/1 bath ranch house in Whitesboro. The houses out there seemed about a quarter mile apart, so different from the subdivision we were used to.

My initial reaction to this 200-yr-old farmhouse could best be described as—well, horrified! It was set on 32 acres, with 2 barns out back (one ready to fall apart), open fields on all sides and woods at the back of the property. The front lawn was very large, the grass was knee-high and it was full of weeds. There were also several tall pine trees with huge trunks and roots that extended several feet out into the lawn, which would later make it difficult to mow. The house? It was a large 2-story home with light green siding, a covered front porch, and French window panes. *"Not too bad"*, I thought.

The inside? Well, to begin with, it had been abandoned the previous fall. As the story goes, the wife of the previous owner had a heart attack while out in the garden and died suddenly. The poor man must've been completely devastated, unable to carry on with even the most basic functions of everyday life. I say this because he had left the house with food in the refrigerator and not only that, his now-petrified dinner in the oven! One can only imagine what condition the rest of this old house was in, but that alone was a good indicator. Although it was August, it felt cold and damp inside and just smelled old and musty. Everything looked just plain old and neglected.

The only downstairs room in good condition was the master bedroom, which had nice, new wallpaper. It had a tall window with a view of fruit trees and what was once a vegetable garden, now overgrown with tall weeds. The wallpaper in the hallway off the kitchen was peeling, and it seemed it had been papered over, and over, and over, and over…there must have been ten layers of wallpaper in that hallway! Upstairs, there was one bedroom to the right that also had new wallpaper, two bedrooms to the left (we had to go through the first to get to the second), one large bedroom straight ahead, and beyond that to the left, a small room which would become our sewing room, and then the 6th bedroom, which would end up being mine. Several of the rooms had unfinished plaster walls and the floors were unfinished, grayed wood. It just looked old, dreary, and dark.

Then we went outside and into the main barn. We weren't able to open the doors on the ground level, so we had to use the ramp to get to the second floor. What we found downstairs was wall-to-wall, knee-deep cow manure—cow manure that had been piling

up for what must've been decades! We older kids knew what all of this meant. There was a *lot* of work ahead, way beyond anything we'd ever imagined. Oh, we were all accustomed to working and each doing our share—and it was a good thing Mom and Dad had always expected that of us, as it would've been much harder to get us to cooperate in this grand endeavor—but in the suburbs it was only general housework. We older kids did a little cooking and baking, mowing a lawn that was only a half-acre, and shoveling the driveway in the winter. Even the preschoolers were expected to do little chores to help. But this?? What were we in for?

Well, despite some of our protests, we did move in. And as the saying goes, "What doesn't kill you makes you stronger". (And it did, so much so that by the time I was 17, I once bench pressed 120 lbs. in our high school weight room, much to the surprise of my male classmates!) We got right to work, banging down some of those old plaster walls and ceilings,  behind which we found old, hard, wood lath. In between the 2-inch slats of wood, we found mortar that was mixed with horse hair. Some of it was broken up and we had to dig it out with putty knives and our fingers. Of course we had to wear dust masks, since we did not know what we would be breathing in! It was very hard, dirty work. We also pulled up the old, worn hardwood flooring in the dining room, using a crow bar to pry up the boards. Under the wood slats, we found piles of what looked like worm skeletons of some sort. We remodeled the kitchen early on so Mom would find it bearable to work in.

We also refinished the downstairs bath off the kitchen. It was in awful condition, as was the kitchen. Dad put in a white porcelain pedestal sink, a new toilet, and white wallpaper flocked with red fleur-de-lis, I think, and also an oval, wood-framed mirror over the sink with antique-looking wall lamps on either side. It seems we kept the existing bathtub. All I really remember about that tub was that the house had sulfur water, (which we'd never even heard of!) and when we'd take a bath, it was like sitting in a big vat of hard-boiled eggs. Needless to say, baths were not exactly something we looked forward to!

Perhaps I should throw in some comic relief at this point. One of my first good memories is sitting on the front porch on a rainy day with only Mom, Dad, Grandma and Grandpa. Dad was telling a story about I-don't-know-what and used the word "intertwingled". He'd meant to say either intertwined or intermingled and just it came out that way. I remember it being one of those times when you just cannot stop laughing!

Funny the things we remember, isn't it? It's also funny the things we forget, and it's intriguing how, although several of us may have been involved in an identical situation, our perspectives are uniquely different. To this day, there's an ongoing difference of opinion as to just how long it took us to empty that one barn of all the manure. I remember it being about 3 yrs or so. Others say it was less, but perhaps they were just too young the first couple of years to do such grueling work.

Imagine that for an after-school chore! The top layer had formed a thick, hard crust. We had to wield a heavy pickaxe to break through it and to break up the manure underneath. It really didn't smell all that bad, surprisingly, but as we broke through that top layer, steam would rise from what was underneath—heavily compacted, brownish-gold manure imbedded with all the undigested hay! We'd then have to use a spading fork and shovel to loosen it and then heave it into the wheelbarrow.

After that, we'd have to wheel it way out to the vegetable garden to the left of the driveway. I remember we owned a manure spreader that could be hitched to the tractor, so either we had it to begin with and it broke down, or we eventually got one. Either way, I do recall struggling to get that heaped-up wheelbarrow over the rocks and bumps and into the garden. On a typical day, we'd be assigned to three or five wheelbarrows full. The priority was to at least clear the area at the back of the barn where the stanchions were. That way we'd have a place to put a cow or two for milking.

I don't remember how long it was before we got our first cow, Red. I was in the barn when she was first delivered, along with Dad and I don't recall who else. Dad, having been raised in an urban area and being new at this thing called farming, didn't realize that cows, like people, don't like to be caught off guard. He reached down, intending to get some milk out of her. Instead he got a good swift kick in the thigh!

He ended up with a long rip in his pants and also a bruised thigh, I'd imagine. A word to the wise—females don't like to be grabbed, and especially not by a complete stranger! Anyway, unlike our second cow, Lady, a very sweet and cooperative animal, Red was a feisty old gal and I was always just a little bit afraid of her. I learned from Dad's experience, though, and would always approach with caution and pet her a little before trying to extract milk out of her. She never did exactly warm up to any of us, but still she did her job and served us well for many years.

Once we had cows, of course, they needed hay to eat for the long, cold winters. Dad bought a baling machine and during the hot summer months, one of us would drive the tractor back and forth and form the bales. Then those of us who were strong enough would lift those 60-lb. bales by the twine and hurl them up onto the wagon. Some of those August days were very hot and humid, but we had to wear long sleeves and pants so the cut hay wouldn't puncture our skin. I just remember being soaked with sweat and very dirty with all the debris from that hay, but there was no getting out of it. It had to be done, so we all worked together and got it done.

Our 1-acre vegetable garden was another grueling, tedious job, at least initially. The soil had not been tilled for a long time, if ever, and it was full of rocks. The only way to get them out was by hand, so that's what we did. Even the little ones could help with that. Eventually, it was ready to be tilled and the seeds planted. In time, we had a big, beautiful vegetable garden on one side of our house and a smaller one on the other. Dad refused to use any chemicals or pesticides and grew it all organically, with only manure to fertilize, as I remember it.

We grew all the usual vegetables, i.e., corn, peas, green and yellow wax beans, carrots, cucumbers, watermelon, pumpkins, potatoes, etc. Oh, and the tomatoes! I remember huge beefsteak tomatoes that were so big and juicy we'd eat them right there in the garden. Another that was fun to eat as we picked was the peas. We couldn't eat too many, though, or we'd end up with a stomachache! We also grew vegetables that none of us kids had ever heard of, like Swiss chard and kohlrabi. Those are two veggies that have only recently begun to show up in the grocery stores and on restaurant menus, so Mom and Dad were way ahead of their time!

Because we grew all our own food, there wasn't much left to buy at the grocery store. All our dairy products came from our two cows, which we milked by machine, and we had plenty of eggs from our chickens. Beside our freezer full of vegetables, which Mom taught us how to prepare for storage, and the tomatoes and pickles she taught us to can, we also had a freezer full of pork and beef. Dad was so proud that we were able to live off our own land and he'd often remark at dinner, "Look at this! Our own steak, our own potatoes, our own peas, our own milk, our own butter..." It seemed it got to be a nightly thing. After awhile, I'd just roll my eyes and think, *"Does he really need to go through this routine every night?"* To quote from a favorite movie of mine, I was "just young enough and just cocky enough to not realize the magnitude of the situation" I was in. Little did I know it, but I was learning

26

values and skills that would benefit me for the rest of my life.

I almost forgot to mention that our old, drafty house was heated by propane. Occasionally, we would have it delivered by truck, but mostly we used wood stoves for heat. We all learned to chop wood, even the skinny pieces used for kindling. Now, that took some effort and a whole lot of perseverance, but there was no getting out of it. We all had to work together and we all were expected to carry our share of the load. Anyway, we only had two wood stoves to heat that great, big house—one in the middle of the downstairs and one in the middle of the upstairs, the room where Christa, Ria and Becky stayed. That meant we all had to keep our bedroom doors open if we wanted any heat in our rooms. Even still, I don't remember it being very efficient, but we survived.

For a time at least, I had the chore of cleaning out the pigpen on Saturdays and I *hated* it. It had to be done or I couldn't go to football games or anything else going on in town. One time, a huge boar—600 lbs., at least!—backed me into a corner of the pen. I was so scared I stabbed him with the pitchfork and it stuck in his skin. Then I had to pull it out! Yeah, of course he squealed, no, screeched! He never backed me into a corner again, though. In fact, because he was so huge, he probably got dragged up the ramp into Dad's pick-up soon after that and got hauled off to the butcher, eventually ending up on our plates—a demise he richly deserved!

As for the chickens, I didn't have much to do with them, other than having to help pluck, gut and cut them up a couple times, which was a really nasty job. I think somehow we just laughed our way through it. What else could we do? Anyway, as much as I didn't like having to clean the pigpen, I was glad I didn't have to clean the chicken coop more than a few times. Their manure smelled awful, way worse than either the pigs or cows! That was a job for Ed, Matt, and Paul mostly.

At the beginning of my story I referred to myself as the black sheep, so now I'll share a few—and only a few!—incidents to illustrate. Needless to say, these were not necessarily funny at the time!

Having had a typical case of FLDD (that's frontal lobe deficit disorder, for any who haven't had adolescents!), I thought it shouldn't be a big deal to smoke in my room at 14. After all, Dad had been a smoker, right? Yeah, ridiculous, I know! Well, that didn't go over so well. Mom caught me and threatened the dreaded, "Wait 'til your father gets home". He came up to my room with two big fat cigars and told me that he and I would smoke them together after dinner. Fortunately (or not) for me, that never happened. He simply left them in one of the little lanterns on the vertical beam between the dining room and kitchen as a friendly reminder. Who knows? Perhaps if he'd followed through, I would've quit right then and there. But probably not.

By the time I was 16, I think, Dad gave in and let me smoke outside. In the winter, I'd stand in that little breezeway off the kitchen—wearing a snowmobile suit at times because it was so cold and blustery outside—and I'd throw my cigarette butts in the snow. Then springtime came and the snow melted. Yup, you guessed it—dozens of butts imbedded in the mud. I had to pry them all up with my fingers. Well, of course! Who else was going to do it? You can bet that never happened again!

Oh, and the wild tractor rides! I remember taking, Ed, Matt, and Paul (aka "the boys"), putting them up on the fenders, and then we'd go tearing through the fields as fast as that old tractor would go. They loved it, especially going over the bumps. One day, though, when we were done with our joy ride, I turned off the key but left it in 4th gear, which is how Dad found it. Uh oh. I got in trouble for that, of course, but it sure was fun! Amazing none of them ever fell off, going over all those bumps at full speed!

Although we all worked hard on our farm, we had our fun times, too. (And no, I'm not referring to chasing pigs down the road when they got out, or searching for cows that had wandered off!) One thing I loved to do was snowmobiling. I remember a couple times going with Dad. He'd take two or three of us way out away from home to some wide open space, load us onto the toboggan and pull us behind the snowmobile—probably a little faster than Mom would've liked, but she wasn't there. Beside, that's what adventurous dads do! We loved it and I know he did too! And—gasp!—we only had the side ropes to hold onto and no seatbelts?! That would be considered negligence by today's over-protective standards, but back then parents weren't so afraid of every little thing that might hurt little Johnny or little Susie.

Mom and Dad also let us make our own mistakes and

didn't always try to protect us from ourselves, unless it was life-threatening, of course! One day after a heavy morning snowfall, I thought it'd be fun to take the snowmobile out by myself. I decided to take it up the big hill behind our property. That trail was well-used by other snowmobilers, so the snow was *usually* packed down and made for a nice, smooth ride. Dad warned me it probably would be impassable, but agreed to let me go. (I think he knew full well I wouldn't make it, but let me figure that out for myself!) The snow was fresh, and it was deep.

Apparently, I was the first to venture out that day because there were no tracks on the hill. Well, I got about a quarter of the way up that hill and got stuck. I shut it off, then lifted the back of the machine and tried to turn it around. Then it *really* got stuck, the front skis firmly planted in the snow bank, the machine at a 45-degree slant. Upward, of course. I tried and tried to move that thing, and it would not budge. Frustrated to tears, I slumped over the seat and sobbed myself to sleep. I'm not sure how long I slept, but when I woke up, I finally mustered the strength and was able to turn that behemoth around and take it back home. Still exhausted, I slept the rest of the afternoon 'til dinner time.

There are many other stories I could tell, but the ones I've told are the memories that left a lasting impression on me. I left the farm in 1977, so the rest of the story will have to be told by the six left at home. Although we didn't realize it at the time, it was a great experience for all of us. It's been said that experience is the best teacher, and I believe far more valuable than *any* academic education. We all learned *so* many valuable skills, such as how to live off the land and be self-sufficient, how to work hard and then enjoy the fruits of our labor, how to get along with others and work together. We were developing values, character traits and a work ethic that would last us all a lifetime, and that we could exemplify to our own children and all those who know us. We learned what truly matters.

32

Ria - Milking, Reading & Sewing

I have mostly pleasant memories of the farm. I recall Dad driving us on the "dirt road" on the way there and the older children complaining that we were headed to the "sticks". I didn't really understand what that meant and I was curious to see where we were going to live. I was very excited to have such a huge house, even though it was messy and needed a lot of work. I always thought Terry's room was a little creepy because it seems like someone said a lady had died there. (The old chimney space in the boys' room was also scary.)

We were so happy to meet the L.'s and find out that they had nine children too. [Several were grown and moved away.] Becky and I became good friends with Sharon and Wendy and had many, many fun days together. I used to daydream that if only I had a pogo stick I could get to the L.'s so much faster! [It was a mile up the road.] I remember crawling through the pipes under the road on the way to their house.

I also remember collecting a bunch of the tar that melted on the edges of the road and making a big ball of it. I put it under my clothes in the back of my drawer to keep it and it made a huge mess. Mom was not happy with me! I could write a whole book on our exploits with the L.'s. (Many songs from the 70's take me back to times with them, so I don't listen to a lot of that because it makes me sad thinking of Clifford and the fun we had driving around the back roads.)[Clifford passed away a few years after we moved.]

Our bedroom had a narrow, deep closet with a sort of cubby in the back. I never understood the purpose of that design. Anyway, I used to take my dog Cleo and a flashlight back in there to read—my favorite thing to do. I'd hear Mom or someone else calling me and I'd just keep on reading. I guess no one ever thought to look there and our clothes hung on spring rods in the front, so I was well hidden.

We had the upstairs wood stove in our room. In retrospect, the boys must have been freezing in the winter! In the spring and summer, when the stove wasn't being used, birds always got caught in the chimney and fell down into the stove. We could hear them inside so we'd open the door and they'd fly around the room until they made it out of the window. Always an adventure!

Speaking of the boys' room, we had a wonderfully fun family game called "Hide Under The Covers." Everyone would get under the blankets on one of the beds in the boys room and the person who was "it" had to feel through the covers and guess who they were touching. We also played a lot of musical chairs with our one and only 45 record, Stevie Wonder's "Superstition". I think Christa and/or I finally bought another 45, Sister Golden Hair.

I think it's funny that we closed up the living room for the winter so we didn't have to heat it. A whole huge room completely unused—did we open it up for Christmas? [Yes.]

I remember the first time Dad sent me out to use the manure spreader. He told me not to turn against the wind. I had no idea what he was talking about, so of course I went up and back then turned against the wind for the third pass and

34

the manure blew all over me! I had to take off my clothes in the breezeway outside the door before Mom let me in the house.

I didn't mind the manure shoveling because we had fun talking when we did it. I can remember the smell, but it was nothing compared to the stench of the chicken coop when we had to clean it in the winter.

And speaking of the chicken coop, one of the nastiest

jobs we had to do was when we had baby chicks. It seemed like there was at least one dead every morning. They piled together to sleep and be warm and they crushed each other to death. We had to move the live ones aside, looking for dead ones and take them out. We must have buried them, but I don't remember that. It was so sad and I can still almost feel their soft bodies, all cold and limp. I won't even go into how much fun it was to pluck the chickens once they were big enough!

In contrast to that, when we had piglets it was so amazing. We had the perfect viewpoint up above the pen where we could look down and watch them. They were so pink and cute, blindly searching for their mother's milk, their umbilical cords all tangled up. I think Terry came home on leave right after they were born. I did not like the pigs much when they were grown because they were very strong and couldn't be easily guided like the cows. We had many days of chasing them when they got out of the pen and it was very annoying.

Christa and I did a lot of the cooking and running the household when we were in our teens [and Mom was at work]. She was more conservative and something of a drill sergeant at the time. (We both are now-ha ha.) When I made breakfast, I took orders and made what everyone wanted. When she made breakfast, everyone got the same thing, usually oatmeal because that was easiest and fastest. Needless to say, I was the favorite cook.

We split the cooking and milking chores, but milking was my personal favorite. I could go out to the barn and be alone with the animals where it was quiet. (I sang a lot.) I liked milking Lady because she was docile and easy. Before I put the machine on her, I hand milked a little for the cats. Red was kind of a pain because she always had a wild-eyed look and had a knack for kicking over the milk bucket just as I was getting done. I learned how to prevent that pretty quickly! In the winter, I put my hands in

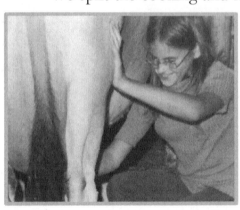

the dip in Lady's side between her pelvis and ribs to keep them warm. I wonder if anyone else did that. It was like a nice warm pocket.

When I was eleven, we went to the W. Farm and picked strawberries. It was our only chance to make money for ourselves, but someone reported us because we were under the eligible working age of 12. The authorities came through and anyone without working papers was told to leave. [I was pretty mad about this too.]

My next job was babysitting for the B's. Probably shouldn't comment on that... They really appreciated my cleaning abilities there!

I worked as a cook at the Gatesdale but I'm not sure how long or what age I was. Probably 16-17 and maybe a year or two. Christa, Lori H. and I worked together there. I can't imagine my children keeping the kind of hours we did. We got up and did the milking, went to school, then worked until 10 or 11. When we weren't working at the Gatesdale, we cooked supper and made sure everything was clean. Somehow we got our schoolwork done and stayed in the Honor Society. I'm sure we were very strict with the boys and Becky at home.

I remember the cellar flooding and having to bail out the water in a bucket brigade. I can still recall the smell of that nasty water. It was kind of a mix of water, oil, mold and concrete.

We had chores after every meal. Mom made lists for us to follow with jobs assigned to each of us. In the summer, we had to do two hours of weeding or garden work every day. One of the gardening jobs was picking the bugs off of the potato plants. We had a little can of gasoline and we picked the bugs off the leaves and put them in the gas. Gross, gross, gross! I can't imagine doing that now!

I did a lot of the butter churning. When I was new at it, I churned in one direction for about five minutes and the cream was thickening up. I turned the churn around to use my other hand and after a few minutes, the cream was back to thin again. It was very strange and I can't imagine why that would happen, but we always churned in the same direction after that.

We took inventory of the freezers and cupboards in the winter. I think that's so funny, actually. Mom gave us paper and a clipboard or something and we went through and counted how many packages of frozen peas, corn, meats, etc. along with jars of pickles, tomato sauce and whatever else we had canned. I would love to have a utility room like that in my house now!

I never liked the closet where the water heater and breakers were because it was slightly dark and I'm pretty sure there were quite a few spiders in there. I think that's where Dad had the container for the elderberry wine he was making.

He also made some very good cheese in a crock. It had a plate or something with a big rock on top of it to press it down I think. [He did make cheese, but the crock was for kapusta—that's Polish sauerkraut]

A couple of first-timer mishaps were with the chainsaw and the snowmobile. At least I think these were me—I have a bad memory so I'm not sure. Dad sent me out to cut down a tree. He explained how to make the cuts and told me to be sure to make the top angled cut first or the saw could get stuck in the tree. So of course I had no idea what he was talking about and I went right up there and got the saw stuck within minutes. He was watching from the window so he came and rescued me. The first time he let me use the Bomber snowmobile, he said not to go too slow or we'd get stuck. Again, no clue as to why/what he was saying, so I went right out and got stuck in minutes. He had to hike up through the snow and get the snowmobile moving again.

I taught myself how to do every craft I could because there wasn't a heck of a lot to do out there. We had no transportation to go anywhere and snow kept everyone inside anyway. I knitted mittens, crocheted (not very good at that) and embroidered (a lost art now). I learned how to operate the sewing machine—how cool to have a dedicated sewing/ironing room! I have an antique White brand sewing machine now that's just like the one we had. It works and I love the way the sound reminds me of sewing in that little room.

People used to give us what Mom called "care packages", which were basically everyone else's cast off clothes. I would look through them for fabrics I liked and take the clothes apart to make them into something else. Mom told me that Grandma said your sewing should look just as good on the inside as it does on the outside, and I still adhere to that. I never leave a hanging thread and finish all of my seams. I think I'm still the expert on sewing zippers in the family even though I got C's in Home Economics class—haha! I got reprimanded for not following the patterns and for not following the recipes exactly when cooking.

I used Vogue magazines to come up with designs for my clothes. I wore skirts to school when no one else did. Even though I often wished I could have the "cool" clothes others had, I also liked being a little different and didn't notice if anyone thought I was weird. I also got my hairstyles from Vogue. I recall wearing a bun on the side of my head to school. Absolutely not cool when everyone else was sporting the Farrah Faucet look!

We went to church in Clayville. Father Baker was fun and nice to us. I loved singing up in the choir loft when I was a teen even though I was the only one there under 60! After Dad died, I drove us to Wednesday night classes there before I had a license to drive. I remember doing that a few times and thinking I might get in trouble, but I'd been driving the tractor for years, so I was a good driver. I learned to drive on the tractor and then drove the red Chevy with the three-speed shifting on the steering column.

I was driving us home one day from church maybe—and when we were going over the top of the hill, suddenly a three-wheeler was flying through the air straight at us. I don't remember whose it was, but it came out of the back of their truck. I can still see that thing coming straight at us. I didn't think at all—just turned the wheel to avoid it and we went bumping off the road and into the field. Very close call!

A lot of my memories are attached to smells: Cow manure always takes me back to milking and cleaning up in the barn. Cut grass reminds me of the haying days. Hay reminds me of swinging on that long rope in the barn. Hay also reminds me of the work of hay baling. Even though it was hard work, I liked those days because we had fun together doing it and then riding home on top of the pile in the wagon. I can immediately identify that sort of sweet scented spray we used on the cows faces to keep flies away. There was an odor in the house that probably came from the wood lath and horsehair plaster walls and the house being closed up for a long time before we moved in—I can't describe it, but every now and then I catch a whiff of something like it and have a memory flash back in time.

Our family wasn't perfect, but Dad and Mom had (have) a strong commitment to the Catholic faith. No matter what, we prayed the rosary together often, and Mom would not let us miss church. I don't know what the others' memories of that are, but I recall it fondly. I remember the dog walking over our legs while we knelt around Mom and Dad's bed and recited all those "Hail Mary's" and "Our Fathers". I liked going to church and enjoyed singing in the choir. I also liked the CCD classes. I think that without those particular things we did together, along with our extended family gatherings, our family would not be as close as we are.

The other thing that comes to mind is that there was no question that Mom and Dad loved each other tremendously. The farm was a catalyst, and our parents' love and faith was the glue. Our spiritual beliefs have taken us down different paths, but we all have faith in God that has carried us through many difficulties in our lives, supported, no doubt, by the many prayers offered on our behalf by our mother.

Ed — Wood, Frogs & the Fish

Wood: We always knew in advance when we'd spend the day up in the woods getting firewood. The day would start out with breakfast which went way too fast because we knew what we would soon face, and it always seemed to be a really nice day...perfect for playing and not so great for humping logs all day that weighed almost as much as we did. Dad would load us up in either the old pickup with the re-purposed manure spreader attached to it or the tractor with manure spreader attached. I think it may have been both depending on where we were going. After all, with the bed of the truck at our disposal we could get that much more in a trip...yay!

(not really, I *hated* getting wood)

Dad would cut down a few trees and then get to cutting them in pieces that we had to load onto the makeshift trailer.

Those darn logs weighed a ton and I think they may have stretched all of our arms by a few centimeters. I remember making sure to wear long sleeves and gloves even when it was warm to protect our arms.

Then there were the wood splitting parties. Dad and Uncle Charley and another of his brothers, probably Uncle Stan, decided to put their heads together and build a wood splitter. The problem was the darn thing worked great...too good in fact, because it never got tired and didn't stop until it ran out of gas or ran out of wood to split. Either way we were dog tired at the end of the day from picking up and stacking

wood and even if there was sunlight left, we were too tired to play. I do recall Dad once running around with us throwing and kicking the football after one of the wood gathering Saturdays.

For the 4th of July, Dad would always buy a big watermelon. One year, he lowered a watermelon into the well in the front yard to keep it cool since I doubt it would have fit in the fridge. We spent the day up at the pond that he had built with a piece of borrowed earth moving equipment. The pond was fed from the stream that came out of the woods and the water was cold! Until we had been in the water for a while and got things stirred up, you could dive off the diving board and the first two feet of water were somewhat pleasant...then

you'd hit the thermal layer and freeze your a- - before quickly heading for the surface. We'd stay at the pond and then have  food and chilled watermelon. I think Allen P. probably came over in the evening with some firecrackers and we would have sparklers and light them up. I'm not sure how many times we did that.

Tracker gets shot: The uncles [Dad's brothers] would always come up around deer season and they would all go up in the woods hunting and it just happened to be around Thanksgiving. I remember checking out their guns thinking they were pretty cool and once saw a little bottle of hooch that I believe belonged to Uncle Stan...he even gave me a swig and I thought it tasted pretty good and if my memory serves me correctly it was blackberry brandy. This particular year, the tree stand/fort was up and I'm pretty sure that's where Dad and the uncles went.

That darn dog [Tracker] was out screwing around with the neighborhood mutts chasing deer and got himself shot. I'm pretty sure it was Mom that said, "go up in the woods and get your father...tell him the dog's been shot." I don't know

 if those were the exact words, but it sounds good to me. Anyhow, as I'm walking toward the barn I'm thinking to myself, "OK, *these guys...as well as a bunch of other yahoos are up in the woods with guns...and at least one of them has hooch. Do I really want to go up in those woods with a bunch of guys with shotguns and buck fever? I think not!"* So I stood at the corner of the barn and just kept yelling for Dad until I saw him come walking out of the woods. I think back now and he must have been p-----d, but I don't remember that being the case. I would've been. Stupid dog.

I remember when Ria got Cleo [after Tracker had died.] She had built a little barrier in her room to keep the dog penned in at night. That dog would jump over it in the middle of the night, and either pee or take a dump on the floor and then climb back over. Ria would get so upset and I remember telling her that Cleo would get out at night, do her business, then look back at her and smile before heading back over the barrier. Just a devious thought from the little brother.

The carp: I remember that like it was yesterday. It was one of those typical upstate New York evenings after it had rained and the sun came out. I remember Dad telling me that he was taking me fishing and I needed to get my "rain gear" together because he thought it might rain again. I was thinking to myself "did he say reindeer?" I didn't know what rain gear was! I didn't have any...turns out it was rubber boots and a raincoat...although I don't remember having a raincoat.

We took off down East Street and crossed Route 20 and drove a bit south. We stopped alongside the road and there was a path there through the woods. We grabbed our stuff and a peanut butter tub full of night crawlers that we had picked some rainy night out in the cow pasture. I specifically remember being out in that pasture with Dad, Becky, and maybe Matt one night. We were out there with a flashlight for what seemed like forever picking those darn worms. They were everywhere too...thousands of them. I believe we filled a 5-gallon bucket with them that night. Dad took a round metal bin and filled it with leaves and dirt and then dumped in the worms where they were stored in the cellar.

...Back to the carp. We made our way down the trail and came to a river (probably a large stream, but when you're a kid everything is big) and started to fish. [most likely the Unadilla River] I think there may have been a bridge to the right of us. We weren't there very long and all of a sudden, my pole bent over. Dad was so excited...he kept saying "let him take it...don't pull too hard or you will lose him". He never took the pole from me, which kind of surprised me. I almost wanted him to so we had a better chance of landing the beast. It felt like I was hooked to a Volkswagen and it kept going back and forth from left to right, but after a period of time I had him on the bank of the river.

I don't think we stuck around after that and we headed home where I posed for pictures with the big catch. I'm pretty sure that fish weighed 10 pounds. Since we didn't eat carp, it ended up buried in one of the gardens. A couple years later when I was in middle school, I saw that path leading into the woods almost daily  on the bus ride. I wouldn't be surprised if it is still there.

Frog legs: One cool, cloudy...very cloudy day I went with Dad to get frog legs. I have no idea where this pond was, but I remember it very well. It did not rain at all that day, but it was dark. The water was almost black and there was dead wood everywhere. To me, it looked like a really good place to fish. We loaded the aluminum boat into the water and Dad steered it around with the little trolling motor he bought for it. We just kind of cruised around the edge of this pond looking for frogs. It was really a large pond...more like a small lake I guess, out in the middle of nowhere.

When we would spot a frog, Dad would shoot it with the old .22 caliber single shot rifle he had. The bullets he used were .22 shorts and after he shot one he would ask for another bullet for the next frog. He would shoot them and then scoop them up with the net. He then took a knife and cut the legs from the body and pitched the carcass into the water for the turtles to eat. That night we had frog legs and they were delish...taste like chicken! That was the only time we ever did that and the only time I remember having frog legs.

Hay: This was another thing I hated. Those stinking bales of hay were so darn heavy...and the sides of the bales were sharp and would scrape the crap out of your arms as you're hefting them on the wagon. I remember one day particularly well. Dad had cut the hay maybe a day or two earlier and this was a Sunday. I'm not sure where Mom was...maybe working, but I remember that Dad went out with the rake to "turn" the rows of hay to help them dry. He knew rain was coming and was afraid of losing the hay so we ended up going out with the bailer and wagon before the grass was really dry enough to be bailed. It is so much worse when the grass isn't dried all the way out because it makes the bales that much heavier. When you only weigh 60 pounds and the bales are 50... well...you get the idea.

We worked all day and managed to get it done and I remember Dad going out during the night a few times to check on the bales in the barn because they could spontaneously combust when they are baled prematurely and wet on the inside. I remember doing that too...sticking my arm down inside a bale and feeling the heat inside of it. Luckily we never had any issues with that. Thinking back now, I realize that is why the bales would sometimes be moldy in the middle when we broke them apart to feed to the cows in the winter. I never really thought about it much back then.

The barn: A beautiful summer day...a Saturday and I'm out mowing the lawn. We had a lot of lawn to mow and I remember how grateful we all were when we finally got a riding lawn mower instead of that hurdy gurdy rotating blade thing that had to be pushed to get the blade to turn. I had been out there for quite a while and mowed the majority of the grass when I noticed the gas gauge was on "E". I turned to head toward the barn to get gas, when I looked up and saw smoke pouring out from the rafters on both sides of the barn...and I mean pouring!

I pushed the throttle to max to get there quicker but instantly realized I could run much faster so I turned the mower off and jumped off and ran toward the barn. At the same time, I'm thinking to myself that I know what is going on up there. I knew Paul and Michael J. from up the road were up there and also knew they had been to the dump earlier in the day with Michael's father. He would go there and look for scrap aluminum and copper and then melt it on a fire in their front yard. Paul and Michael had picked up cigarette butts they found in a pile and brought them back with them.

As I got in the barn, I noticed a garden hose snaking its way up the stairs to the hayloft and that just confirmed what I already knew. I ran up the stairs and the entire loft was full of white smoke. I could see light from the flame, but nothing else and I could hear the crackling from the fire. I yelled at them and asked them what was going on and Paul said "The barn's on fire!" Yeah...no s--- the barn is on fire... because you two fools are up here monkeying around. (I didn't say that, but probably thought it.) I yelled to them "Let's go, we gotta get out of here!" and they came to the stairs and down we went. I can only imagine they heard my voice and it guided them to the stairs because visibility was zero.

We ran to the house and I caught Mike and Mom who were just getting ready to leave to go somewhere and told them the barn was on fire. As someone called the fire department, Mike and I ran to the side doors of the barn and Mike opened them. We grabbed the snowmobiles and pulled them out as far as we could and Mike grabbed one of the fire extinguishers that was sitting there. He tried to use it and the water came out of it like a pee stream...pretty much useless.

The fire department came, but with an all-volunteer department and us living in the sticks, the response time isn't the greatest. By the time they arrived it was ready for marshmallows. The ironic thing was, there are no fire hydrants there so they ended up going to the pond behind the J.'s house to suck up water into the fire trucks to put on the fire.

52

I remember one of the girls, maybe Ria, had to keep the cows away because they kept trying to get into the barn while it was burning. I also remember standing at the back of the house watching and remember feeling the heat from the fire. Even at that distance it was intense. I went into the barn with Mike a day or two later to see if anything was salvageable. The aluminum ladders were melted into chunks of aluminum. The mowers that I used to tear apart that were on the second floor were piles of molten metal. Only a few things in the front of the barn on the ground floor were able to be used. The chicken coop survived, but I think at this point we had gotten rid of those filthy animals.

The chickens: Dad bought either 100 or 200 little yellow chicks. I remember thinking how cute they were... that is until those rotten birds got big and crapped all over the place. Cleaning the chicken coop was the worst job on the farm. It reeked liked no other... even the day after it was cleaned. To this day I despise birds...they are filthy creatures.

I was not the least bit upset when Dad would tie their filthy little legs to the fence and cut their necks when it was time for plucking and freezing...and the plucking just added to my disdain for them. That was nasty too...stunk like no other. The girls all in their plucking get-ups...Mom throwing them in hot water to loosen the feathers...pulling those stinky feathers out. Rotten they are.

I think I recall Dad and Don killing a pig once and hoisting it up in the same tree that I climbed when Christa shot at me with the .22. I'd forgotten that until someone reminded me of it a few years ago.

As for other life on the farm, I don't remember really specific things…mostly just in general terms. For all I know, I may have imagined all of it!

Matt — Fishing, Work & the Pond

I have a lot of memories of the farm. Most of them were the best times of my life. We moved there when I was very young. My earliest recollection is that we originally had two barns and Dad demolished one of them although I'm not sure why. [It was dilapidated and a hazard.] About this time, I also remember Babci [Grandma, in Polish] was there one time and we had a lot of flies there so we also had a lot of the flypaper hanging in the house. I remember one of them getting caught in her hair!

As everyone knows it was a lot of work on the farm, but I did like a lot of that work. When it was wood season I liked that because we worked together like a team stacking and loading it. I thought it was a lot of fun most of the time. Dad did a great job teaching us teamwork and I always felt I was getting physically stronger working with the wood, chopping, splitting and stacking it.

It was also very exciting to me because we did most wood cutting in the fall and that was my favorite season. The way the air smelled, the changing of the leaves, the colors—it's always stuck with me and I miss it. [Matt lives in a big city now.]

Another thing that's always stuck with me was a well-deserved whoopin' I got once while we were all in the woods working. Dad was backing up our old Ford 800 tractor to hook up to the wood wagon and I wanted to cross to the other side and decided it was OK to take a shortcut between the moving tractor and the parked wagon. Not too wise; Dad

55

parked the tractor immediately and cut a switch from a tree and I got a good whoopin'. Later on, he explained to me that it was a dangerous thing that I did and that I could've been crushed. One of the few times Dad explained a whoopin'! Needless to say, lesson learned.

Most years I pretty much hated winter because we were stuck inside a lot of the time because of the bitter cold. Some winters were harsher than others and we hadn't planned for it so we ended up having to get more wood—in the dead cold of winter, which was not fun at all! Some years we couldn't even go to family functions because the snow was so bad. I

remember shoveling out the driveway at night because Mom was coming home from working the 3 to 11 shift at the hospital. Dad had a bunch of change in that little plastic change thing that he carried in his pocket and gave it to me as a reward. [We normally didn't get paid for chores. Room and board was our pay. There was no such thing as an 'allowance'.] I also recall the snowplow filling in the end of our driveway many times as soon as we were finished shoveling it! Although there were good times—sledding, skating and snowmobiling, I can do without the snow and cold. Besides that, there are other fun things to do without the snow.

Another season I really liked was spring. The snow melted and the weather starting to get warm. The flowers were blooming and there were a lot of birds outside and everything began to have life again. It was also the time we began to tap the maple trees for sap to make syrup. That was also pretty cool, but as I remember also a lot of work, however it was worth it.

Trout fishing season in New York started on April 1st. I always really enjoyed fishing with Dad and then again when I got a little older by myself. One year on the first day of trout season, I was fishing at the river on the dirt road. I was standing on the bank and there was still snow on the ground and a lot of it. The bank gave way and I fell into the icy river. Man was it cold!!! I walked home as fast as I could in the snow, freezing. (Another reason why I don't like the cold and the snow.)

I do, however, like it when it rains. Especially in New York where we lived. When it rained a lot, we used to go outside at night and find night crawlers—awesome bait for fishing. I remember one time Ed, Paul and I decided to go camping in the woods. It rained really hard the first night and we got soaked by the rain because the tent we were in wasn't very water resistant. It was really stormy. We decided to go home and Dad teased us for not being able to handle it.

I remember a time when I was about 12 years old and decided to go fishing and I left early in the morning. I went to a few different spots but the fish weren't biting. I finally ended up at a pond on the property of Ed P. It started to rain a little bit and the trout were biting like crazy and I caught a lot of them. It was getting dark so I decided to head home, but I decided to first stop by Mr. P.'s place to show him my catch. He told me that Mom had called him worried because I wasn't home all day and it was almost dark. He said he was

about to call a search party for me. Mom wasn't very happy with me, but I didn't understand what all the fuss was about because I was used to going fishing. I guess I just didn't normally stay out that long—anyway I was just growing up and trying to be a man—after all, I was 12 years old!

I also remember the pond Dad made. The first one had a standpipe that was too high and it rained really hard one night. Because the overflow pipe was too high, the dam broke and most of the water ran out into the cow pasture. I was with Dad when he was changing the pond and putting in a shortened standpipe. I was sitting on the tractor with him using the back blade to dig it out.  All of a sudden Dad turned the tractor off and told me not to talk. There were some deer that came to the edge of the woods to graze and they just stared at us for what seemed like hours, although it was probably only minutes. I remember that like it was yesterday.

Hay season was always fun for me. I loved it—the smell of fresh-cut hay reminds me of the farm. I'm sure Mom and Dad didn't like it as much because it was a lot of work for them and I also remember them getting hay fever.

We had a feral cat

running around on the farm and he was really mean. It seems no one could catch him. One morning Mom was milking the cows and I think she tried to catch him. I don't know if he scratched her or bit her but he really did a number on her hand. I just wanted to kill that cat for hurting Mom. Justice was served because I think he was the cat that was killed in the barn fire.

I have another experience of milking the cows. One morning I was milking Red or Lady and she picked up her leg and stepped on my foot with her hoof and broke the baby toe on my left foot. And who can forget getting swatted in the face with the cows' tails while they were swinging them to get the flies off of them?

I also remember plucking chicken feathers and how Mom and the sisters all wore bandanas and I think most of them were disgusted by the whole ordeal. I suppose if it wasn't for the brutal winters I might live there again. Beats the heck out of living in the city!

Christa — Demo Days, Decorating & Dad

We didn't see Grandma and Grandpa very often, but I remember a time on the farm when they came to visit. I don't think we had been there very long. We had torn down the wall between the kitchen and dining room. I was there when Mom took a crowbar to the wall with many a "take this Michael", "Take that Susan" as she hit the wall. Joking of course! Once that was all one room, Dad wanted to take out the old tongue and groove floor. I remember him there with Grandpa prying up the floor and underneath there were bunches of dried up curly black worms. Fascinating! I guess Grandpa was a perfectionist and I can remember vague discussions about how the whole project would go. At the same time I remember making egg sandwiches with chives from our garden.

There was a well in front of our house. Mike built a stone housing with a roof for it. Very cool. The well water was an even 42 degrees all year round, so we were told. All that changed when lightning struck our sulfur well or the pump for that well. [Our deep

well and main water source.] For a while, in order to get water for dishes and laundry or whatever, we took the wagon and tractor up to the pond and filled 5 gallon buckets to pour in the front well. The well water never seemed the same after that.

Dad wanted to do things "the old way" so we got a cow. He tried to hand milk Red who promptly kicked him and ripped his pants all the way down the leg. Hence the milking machine. Does anyone remember what a surcingle is? Then there was a hand crank butter churn. Churning butter was a regular after school chore. Then came the hand crank cream separator. Remember the 13 "discs"? They were cone shaped metal parts where the cream would get stuck when you had to wash them. We also had a hand crank ice cream maker. Strawberry was a favorite!

We had huge gardens—fertilized by the composted manure which filled the barn and which we shoveled out by hand. Dad believed in organic gardening. We grew all kinds of vegetables—some experimental like rutabagas, parsnips and kohlrabi. He would sit at the dinner table (an old castoff lab table procured from Griffiss Air Force Base I think) and remind us of all the things we were eating that we had produced.

Mom worked on her decorating skills. We bought many rolls of 39-cent wallpaper at the general store in town. If the wallpaper sheets didn't quite meet or we missed a spot, Mom would say, "That's ok…just put furniture in front of it." It became a running joke. She also "antiqued" a lot of furniture—green, red, yellow and blue antiquing comes to mind. Must be where I get my interest in faux finishes!

We rarely had company when we lived on Butternut Circle, but when we moved to East Street it seemed as if everyone wanted to visit—especially at suppertime. 5PM! We finally changed Sunday supper to Sunday dinner after church [at noon]. I remember coming home to the smell of a roast cooking in the crock-pot. Yum. And we always had some kind of pie or cake for desert. It was a rare supper that was not followed by some type of dessert.

We had a party line on our telephone, which meant that although we had separate numbers, if a neighbor needed to use the phone they would just pick up and we had to get off the phone. Our neighbor, Jerry P., just liked to pick up his phone and listen to our conversations!

I remember a discussion about hooking up the washer

and dryer. It was finally determined that we would have a washer, but clothes would hang on a line to dry, which was fine if it's summer but in the winter we would hang clothes in the utility room and also in the attic. When we went to get them off the line in the attic they would be stiff and frozen.

Microwaves did not exist. How did we survive? Nor did VCRs. The Internet. Cellphones. CDs. Or even the Walkman. Cable TV was just getting to Utica but we had only 3 channels on our TV. I remember watching Barnaby Jones when Grandma and Grandpa came to visit. Regular shows included Hogan's Heroes and Saturday cartoons with Fat Albert at noon. Mom and Dad would watch Johnny Carson. I used to watch black and white old movies at 1 pm.

Mom grew delphinium (larkspur) by the garden in the front. And coreopsis in front of the barn. And sunflowers. There were peonies in the front yard. I used to sit in a chair in the living room looking out the window across the field. I could watch a good thunderstorm roll in across the field toward the house.

One time when I was 12, Mom and I were heading to Bridgewater. We went down the "dirt road" (the same one we were brought to the farm on) in the Volkswagen bug. It was a rough ride. When we got to route 8 the ride was a little smoother until all of a sudden one of the wheels flew off into a field. Stripped it right off the bolts! Mom managed to keep control of the car and pulled over to the side of the road. Jim W. walked out of the field carrying the wheel. Somehow through that I ended up picking strawberries for Jim for 2 summers.

There was a cemetery on East St. about a half mile from our house. We used to go walk through and scare ourselves and each other. There was one grave of a guy named Jabez. I don't remember all but it read. "Here lies Jabez...The stones were crooked. Some were falling over. No one had taken time to clean it up in many years. Periwinkle covered much of the cemetery.

When Dad decided to get pigs we started with three. The four oldest had to draw straws to see who would care for them first. I drew the short straw. I cried. We had to feed them for a week then clean the pen on Saturday. I was scared because they were big and snorted.

The following story isn't a happy one, but I thought it should be included as it is part of our lives. I was 17 so I remember some of it quite vividly. Dad had his first heart attack when he was 48. I remember visiting him at St E's [Hospital]. I think Ria was with me. He had saved his dessert for us. It was scary because I had never been in a hospital past the ER, but Mom seemed to know a lot of people. Becky made a welcome home banner for him. I remember

Dad stayed home from work for awhile after that. He used to sit in the dining room by the stove in a chair that the dog, Tracker, would steal as soon as he got up. Dad might have been in the hospital for a  while that time because I had to cook supper a lot. I made liver and squash because I liked it and because there was a lot of it in the freezer! I guess I must have been pretty bossy over the younger siblings because I remember Mom telling me something like "we're the parents and you don't need to worry about what the younger kids are doing!"

Dad had to retire due to his health in 1978. I thought it was weird, but Dad would watch *Days of Our Lives* and give me the update when I got home from school. Weird because soap operas were not his kind of thing. He wore brown pajamas and a blue plaid bathrobe.

I remember clearly the day Dad had the last heart attack. It was a nice day. Sunny. Fall. I knew he did not feel well. I knew Mom had called the ambulance. She told me to go pick tomatoes in the garden...the one on the opposite side of the house from the door. Dad sat on the steps and waited for the ambulance. It seemed like a long time. I did not see the ambulance but there was a neighbor there to help. I do not know who it was. Could have been Edie B. I remember

Mom later saying that she could have driven Dad to the hospital faster because the ambulance was on another call. I do not know where anyone else was at that time.

Dad died October 12, 1978. The four oldest of us went to the hospital to see him. Our long-time friends, the B's were there. Some aunts and uncles. He was on a ventilator. Not responding. I went to school the day after that visit. I was called to the principal's office and told by someone there that Dad was gone. I went back to Physics class. When I went home Mom gathered all of us together to tell us. She apologized to Matt because we would not be able to celebrate his birthday, which was the next day. The funeral was on a rainy day. We had to go to the funeral home near Holy Trinity then drive all the way to Clayville to the cemetery.

I guess I could probably write a whole book of things that happened on the farm. Some things are as vivid as yesterday. Some memories are a whole story and some are just an impression. I think it was a very impressionable age for most of us as well as the last time the whole family was together.

68

Paul — Fun, Names, & the Barn

I have several fond memories of life on the farm. This will be just a collection of random thoughts and memories. I don't remember moving there but I do remember how big the house seemed, and going back years later, it was much smaller than I remembered. I remember crawling around in every nook and cranny of the house, especially behind the attic stairs where we found the old autograph book— that was really cool. I recall how Mike re-did the walls in his bedroom with wood siding.

We all thought it looked really cool, though we were not allowed in there. I remember shooting the BB gun at a pillow in that room, and then dad dismantling said BB gun on an old beer keg or something. It was all Ed's fault.

Also there was one time when I got an electric shock and I was accused of pulling a plug out from the cord, which I usually did but not on this occasion. No one showed any mercy.

I also remember the time when I was diligently cleaning

my bedroom and removed one of the floor registers, had to run downstairs for something really quick, stepped in the floor duct, and having strategically positioned a chair in the way, landed my face directly on it. I was crying like a baby, more because I broke my tooth than the pain of it all. Of course the ribbing had to follow: snaggle tooth, chipped tooth, etc. mostly from Matt, who also came up with clever names after the barn incident, which I will get to later.

Every time Mom went off to work, she always had the same sort of smell—probably hairspray and perfume—and she always dabbed her lipstick off on a piece of toilet paper. I'm reminded of that any time I smell Breck hairspray. I remember she always gave me aspirin crushed up in honey when I was sick to make me feel better, and would feed it to me by the spoonful. It's good to be the baby.

One time on the 4th of July, Dad had set off a bunch of fireworks for us while Mom was at work. Then we went to bed and Mom came home, but Dad had saved the best ones, which were Roman candles, for her for a private fireworks show. Of course we weren't sleeping and had to watch out the window. There was another time when we boys were working with Dad around the tractor and he "cut the cheese". He looked around at us, and said "somebody peeped". We all got the giggles.

I remember the gardens and how proud Dad was of everything. As we sat down for dinner he would talk about *our* peas, or *our* corn. After growing my own, I understand the pride. Cleaning the chicken coop is a smell that will never be

forgotten. I remember helping with the hay baling which was really hard work, so I didn't have to do much because I was so small, [Too Small Paul is one of his nicknames.] but that did not get me out of chopping wood, and more wood, and more wood.

I remember using those little aluminum tubes and buckets to collect the maple sap, and then Dad making gallon after gallon of maple syrup, which had that nice flavor but it's really hard to come by. I think he used half of a 50 gallon drum or something to cook it in. It had to be cooked for a long time but it was delicious. I also remember the time we collected about 30 burlap bags full of apples from the woods, took them to Fly Creek Cider Mill and ended up with somewhere around 25 gallons of apple juice/cider. We really didn't know how good we had it back then.

Who else remembers the "manure tea" that we put on our plants? It was kept in a barrel by the cherry tree. The gardens require a second mention, because they were amazing. And it was really special when Dad decided to put in the orchard and we had everything we could possibly need. Dad's CB handle of *Green Thumb* was quite appropriate. I still can't get over the courage it must have taken to move from the city, decide you're going to be a farmer and do it, and do it well.

One time, Ed got upset about something and bailed off to the woods. He had on a red parka so Mike called him Little Red Runaway. I also remember our first camping trip; I think

it was the three boys. We loaded up our stuff and headed off into the woods and set up camp. We thought we had everything we needed, but we were unprepared and got hungry and wanted some hot dogs or something else. I apparently was the chosen one, went back to the house and got caught sneaking back into the house grabbing a cookie. I cried. I think I did that a lot.

I remember in the wintertime going sledding down Beringer's Hill, the dirt road down the street. We had the roll-up red sleds. After a while, we needed some more excitement, so we decided to build a ramp at the bottom. After a few hard landings we figured we should go home and get some pillows, which we did, to soften the blow. On one occasion, Matt was dragging up a runner sled and I was going down in another type and we collided. I think I got a mild concussion, and I remember vividly there was a chunk of bloody snow hanging off my eyebrow. It really freaked me out, so I cried. The winters there were especially fun, as a kid with no worries. I remember going out till I was blue in the face, fingers and toes frozen, and would come inside and lay out all our wet stuff out on the downstairs stove and hang around it to warm up.

Who else remembers having shoveled out the entire driveway all the way to the street, only to see Don M. come rolling up on his tractor with the snow blower attached? I have a feeling Dad was on the phone and the conversation was something like, "OK Don, they're almost done, you can come on down." One cool thing he did was piling up snow all in a mountain out by the street and I remember building snow forts in there. I only recall one bad storm, or rather the aftermath, where snow

was halfway up the door on the side porch. Pretty sure that was a snow day. I recall on that and other cold days, Michael bringing the battery in from the car so it wouldn't be frozen the next day, and one particular time, he came in with icicles on his mustache.

I had a lot of fun in the woods, spent a lot of time there. I remember building a log cabin style fort only a couple feet high, digging out the soil and covering it with moss. I was proud of that. I also remember one year when I went out to the woods with a hand saw and climbed to the top of one of the tallest pine trees I could find that looked pretty good, sawed off the top of it, and dragged it back to house to use as a Christmas tree. I'm not sure whether we used it or not, I think it was kind of raggedy by the time I got it back home.

I also remember the time that Becky broke the front skis on the snowmobile trying to go up the side of the bank at the pond. [Dad was gone by then and there was no one and no money to fix it so we never used it again.] Speaking of the pond, that was a really fun place. I remember mucking around in the edges of it, digging down in the grime, pulling up whatever little insects I could find, or catching frogs.

And who can forget blueberry picking? We'd have an eighth of a bucket, Dad's would be overflowing. Our lips would be blue and our bellies full. It was on those days we were grateful that Dad installed the second bathroom!

As for certain family events, I remember one Christmas when Terry had come home and she brought gifts. I could not tell what was in mine it was driving me nuts. Something in it rattled around and made some noise. I got so frustrated

I said to her that if they were rocks I'd throw them at her, probably egged on by my brothers. It turns out that they were army guys, and I felt like such a fool. Then of course Michael's comment about Christa: She came downstairs one morning in a bathrobe and her hair was kind of spiky and Mike call her Chris-Tush, the Queen of Country Punk. But mostly I remember her being bossy.

One time when Susan was out on the porch smoking, she invited us to join in. She said take a really big breath, and of course we turned green in the face and started hacking.

I remember both Ria and Rebecca got their kicks out of dressing me up like a girl. One Halloween we had a costume party at the L.'s. Matt was dressed up as the groom; I was dressed up as the bride. We won first place, a big huge lollipop! In their defense, they did a lot of fun things with us and kept us occupied, like playing cards and board games. They always seemed to be together, thick as thieves.

On one occasion on the school bus, Ria had made a plaid cape with a hood & one of the girls waited until the B.'s got off the bus and asked her "How far did you have to chase a n***** to get that?" On my way off the bus (it must have been winter time), I had my scarf kind of balled up and bopped it in the girl's face. We had never heard such an expression and couldn't believe she would say that! And how about the gown that Ria made out of the curtains!

Ed and I tormented poor Matt, because he had a little more meat on his bones then we did. We called him gut, guttles etc. I'm sure some of you remember the chant, "fat hog of a liar if he sits on you you're through". It seems we came up with some funny jingles. We were merciless.

Mike used to throw the football around for us all the time, got us to go really deep and throw a long bomb. Also his telling us to "mind your deportment" sticks out quite a bit. The most poignant memory of Mike, however, was after the barn incident. I was in the dining room near the kitchen table, and he came around the table toward me and I thought I was going to get smacked. Instead he put his arm around me and told me everything was going to be OK. (Sniff, sniff).

The only specific item I recall about Mom was

when she got to drive the tractor for the first time. She had a smile from ear to ear. Also the ridiculous songs she would sing when she was trying to wake us up in the morning, old-timey stuff. [I don't know the morning song, but here's a sample of others she sang: Be careful crossing streets, ooh-ooh, Cut out sweets, ooh-ooh, Lay off meat, ooh-ooh, You'll get a pain and ruin your tum-tum! Eat an apple every day...And then there's: Getting to know you, Getting to know all about you. Getting to like you, Getting to hope you like me.]

Dad used to have interesting sayings such as: *You know why I call you Sonny, because you're so bright.* That, and *I'll give you a reason to cry.* He would try to do something special for us on our birthdays. I remember going to the corner soft serve ice cream place and getting blackberry ice cream.

One time Grandma and Grandpa came to visit, and Grandpa and I were talking about school. He asked me what my favorite subject was and I said math. He said I like figures...the figures on the beach.

It was always fun to have the city slickers come to the farm. They were so out of their element, especially their distaste for our water, which they claim tasted like rotten eggs. I was used to it and couldn't smell it, and the city water tasted like chemicals to me.

Once I was at the M.'s playing with the kids there, and decided to show the M. boy (I forgot his name) how to throw someone over your shoulder, which I did. He landed funny and hurt his back and I got in trouble over that one.

There was one time I wanted to make a lamp for

Grandma. It was recommended that I go to the neighbor, so I went over and Jerry helped me build this neat little lamp which I think is still around. We always thought those people were kind of weird eating bean sprouts and that sort of thing. Speaking of bean sprouts, I'll never forget the old lady at the end of the road who paid us to mow her lawn. She would offer us all kinds of weird foods and snacks and make sure we wore a bandana on our head so we wouldn't get sunstroke. I think she paid 5 dollars to mow that yard.

We also spent a lot of time playing and hanging out at the H.'s. We had some really good ball games in their front yard. There was one time I was up to bat, hit a line drive straight into Steve S.'s glove. And next time up to bat, another line drive straight into Steve's glove (he was pitching). I didn't have many people my age to play with around there. However there was Michael J. Which leads me to the following story: The Barn Incident of '79.

It was a cool breezy day in the spring of '79, May I think. Michael J. and I were goofing around at his house, probably dragging snapping turtles out of their pond. Mike came from kind of a poor family and his parents really didn't care what he did and he didn't have a great upbringing. Also, both of his parents smoked. We came across an ashtray with several partially burned cigarettes, and thought it would be pretty cool to take the tobacco out and burn the tobacco. So we scraped out a pretty decent pile and decided it'd be a good idea to take it up to our house and do it there.

We headed on up to the house and figuring no one would see us in the barn, that's where we went. We heated up a little pile on the second floor over near the side wall facing the P.'s house. After several attempts to get it going we decided it was too breezy there and had to come up with another plan. We looked around and noticed the hay bales were built in kind of a box fashion and said to ourselves, "There's no wind up there, it would be perfect." So we climbed up in the hay box and continued our ill-fated experiment. It was pretty neat for a couple seconds until the hay caught fire. Flames started shooting up and we jumped out of there. I ran downstairs as fast as I could and filled a bucket partially with water, ran back up and tried to douse the flames.

Realizing that wasn't good enough, I ran back down the stairs and dragged the hose up, but by then the entire pile of hay was on fire and I panicked. I ran back to the house as fast as I could ever remember running. Mike J. ran home. By then, the smoke must have been pretty thick and someone had called the fire department. It's mostly a blur after that. Consequently I was not allowed to see Mike for quite some time after that.

I'm happy to report that although this was the most traumatic event of my life, it did yield some wonderful new names, mainly from Matt. Torch, torque, barn burner, you name it, I heard it. "Were you born in a barn or did you just burn one down?" Karma I guess.

Seriously though, although I could go on for days, I can't imagine having grown up anywhere else or with a more wonderful family. We shared love and memories most will never know. We worked hard, played hard, and ate like kings

79

(from our garden, which we grew ourselves). We had better parents than we deserved, especially Mom who has weathered more storms than anyone should have to. We were truly blessed, our cup truly "runneth over!"

Mike — Wishing Well, Projects & Cold

After we moved in there was some deal with the real estate agent, and he paid for a family dinner at a nice restaurant in town. It was the only time the entire family went out to dinner together.

There was a motorcycle hill climb each September just down the road on East St. which drew quite a crowd. We could hike through the woods to watch. Some of the girls would watch from the L.'s house which was pretty close to it. Bikers came from all over the Northeast to see who could make it up the 480 foot hill in the shortest time (around 10 seconds.) The crowd wasn't the type Dad wanted us hanging around. After a few years that excitement was over when the bikers found some new hill to climb.

Early on, I made the stone wishing well in the front yard. For the roof I used weathered barn wood from the old hop barn that we later tore down. Previous owners had grown or stored hops in it sometime in the past, so we always called it the hop barn. The water from this well was very cold and we used a hand

pump to draw the water. It wasn't sulphur water. During summer the younger kids used the well water to have water wars.

I also made the flagpole surround with stone, chain links and small posts for the huge flag we flew that had covered Dad's casket. Mom filled the center with red and white petunias.

I used the wood from the hop barn to panel the walls in my bedroom. I learned taxidermy and stuffed a squirrel, deer head and various other small animals. Becky made a pencil drawing of the squirrel (that she still has) when she was in high school.

I moved away in May of 1974 to College Park, MD. But after Dad had a heart attack, I was around from Sept. '74 to spring of '75, then back to MD until Dad died in October '78. I decided Mom would need me to help out for a while. There was never much work in the area, no matter what I had studied or what I was looking to do.

There was a large tree alongside the driveway with a thermometer. On Christmas Day of 1978, the temp was -35 without any wind; it was dead still. That's 35 degrees BELOW ZERO. We brought all the batteries inside to warm up so we could start the vehicles. When it finally got up to 10 degrees, it felt warm!

 I did a lot of snowblowing and shoveling. The snowblower was a Jacobsen, 30 inch cut. It would always start no matter what, even after having been idle for a couple weeks in near zero temperatures. We had quite a long driveway and I heard it quit running once I left. Poor youngsters!

The tractor was a different matter. It used an old 6-Volt system and often refused to cooperate; however, once running it rarely skipped a beat. The bulldozer that was digging the pond got stuck and needed a larger piece of equipment to free it.

We used Uncle Charley's wood splitter once the trees were cut and brought down near the barn. We could put an enormous log into it and the splitter could make short work of it. Everyone gathered around to watch the fun. Believe me, it was fun seeing that we didn't have to hand split all of the wood. Some kinds, like oak, are very difficult. We did, however, continue to hand split the kindling and also the other wood when the splitter wasn't available to us.

When the barn fire broke out we called the FD, which was all volunteers, and then scrambled to get stuff out of the barn. The hose didn't work more than a dribble so we were spectators. The entire rear of the barn was a wall of fire, ground to roof.

[I wanted to add some more details to Mike's story, he seems to have a selective memory. He was the hero of all of us younger kids when he was around. He would sometimes play ball with the boys and me, with enough begging. Sometimes it was hitting the baseball to all of us in the outfield. In the fall it would be throwing the football to us. Mike could really throw it long! One time we were all playing in the house, tossing the ball around, and Mike hit the light fixture on the ceiling with his hand going for a high ball, and he broke it. But Mike never got in big trouble for it; he was too old. Mom or Dad just scolded him for playing in the house. Some years later, Mike was just goofing around, throwing pinecones up at the house. Later on, for some reason I threw a rock up and cracked one of the windows. When it was discovered, I let Mike take the blame, because I knew he would just get away with it. He didn't know whether he had done it or not.

I also loved watching football with Mike. I had to ask lots of questions, but eventually I had it figured out. By late high school, I could throw a pretty long pass myself! We had a long running feud between the Dallas Cowboys fans and the Pittsburg Steelers

fans in our house. I was for the Steelers and Ed and Mike were for the Cowboys. Of course we also rooted for our New York teams. The New England Patriots were pretty terrible in those days.]

86

Becky – Garden, Spiders & Walks

One of the earliest repair jobs I remember is Dad patching the roof of the barn. Dad was wisely tethered to the roof by a rope that went over the roof and across the pig yard. I don't know what it was anchored to, but it was a little too low. Dad was working away when all of a sudden he was being yanked like a marionette on the tin roof and he hollered for help. It turned out a pig had gotten

BEFORE AND AFTER ROOF REPAIR

tangled up in the rope and was trying to get loose! That was a close call!

We had two large gardens for our own produce. We were organic gardeners before it was the cool thing to do. One particular summer, Dad assigned the boys and me to picking potato beetles off the potato plants. We each had a small soup can of gasoline and he showed us how to pick them and drop them in the can. Ewww! Is that even organic gardening? There is no way I would do that, but of course I

87

couldn't tell Dad that. As soon as he walked away, I made some kind of deal with the boys and never touched one bug.

The gardens were very abundant and our jobs involved constant weeding, watering and eventually harvesting. Every year we filled a large chest freezer with vegetables, and with wild berries picked from all around the area. We would get permission from other landowners to pick the long forgotten berries on their land. Here's a list of the produce we grew annually:

- Green beans - the bush variety. All beans had to be snapped into 2-inch segments
- Yellow wax beans
- Peas - lots of pea shucking on hot summer days
- All kinds of squash
- Corn - always a highly anticipated favorite
- Carrots - you can leave them in the ground and cover with thick layer of hay and pull them out in the middle of winter
- Potatoes
- Turnips - once or twice (no one liked them)
- Beets
- Tomatoes - all kinds; we canned around 100 jars each year
- Cucumbers - pickling variety. We pickled about 100 jars, mostly dill, but we did make some sweet pickles and bread and butter pickles

- Cabbage - for making kapusta!

- Lettuce - usually leaf varieties. Head lettuce went to seed too fast

- Radishes

- Sugar beets - once or twice. I have no idea what we did with these, but they grew huge. See a picture in Paul's story.

- Last, but not least-horseradish - great for those Easter eggs!

We also had fruit trees already growing on the property when we bought it:

- Cherry-the yellow and red kind

- Pears-hard and crunchy

- Crab apples

- Apples

We got a lot of milk from just two cows and always drank whole, unpasteurized milk. Dad bought a pasteurizer but by that time we were used to raw milk and didn't like the taste. We had a separator for the milk, and Dad mounted it on a bench that we could straddle and sit on while we cranked. The separator is made up of literally a million parts. (Don't you hate when people say literally when it's not? We were always sticklers for spelling and grammar—some worse than others. "The treacherous army of grubs retraced their steps over Pinochle Hill for the analyzation of the Pooze pools." Only family will get that one—a sentence made up to mock one sibling's vocabulary faux pas. There's another error in this paragraph; I left it for the sticklers!)

Back to the separator: The "discs" are a stack of 10 or 12 cone shaped parts with a hole in the center that had to be in the correct order for it to work, so they were kept on a sort of giant safety pin whenever the separator wasn't in use. After separating the milk, you put them on the safety pin and then had to wash all the parts. Washing everything was the worst part of the job. At some point, the part that the discs connected to on the machine got lost. It was never found again.

We skimmed the milk by hand for a while, which got old fast, and eventually, I think it was Uncle Charley who made a new part. I thought this was ingenious since he didn't have the original part to use as a pattern. He worked at some shop that had metalworking machines. The part didn't look quite like the original, but it saved the day for us, because it was an old machine and we could not locate a new replacement part. I was always intrigued by how the machine could take whole milk and turn it into skim milk and cream in minutes. It seemed like a miracle to me. How does it do it? Something to do with centrifugal force, I imagined, as I sat there cranking the handle.

We also hand-cranked all of our own butter, and occasionally in the summer we got to make ice cream, which was a real treat. I don't know why we didn't do it more often since the cream was essentially free. Maybe it was too much work after all the other required jobs! Butter was more yellow in the summer when cows were eating fresh grass.

Every year we bred our 2 milk cows with beef cattle and they produced young ones to be slaughtered when grown. (I first decided I did not want to be a vet when I observed the process of artificial insemination, and saw the long rubber glove that protected his entire arm during the process. My decision was solidified when I saw how the rubber bands were used on the male calves!) I think the calves were on a rotating schedule and we had one animal slaughtered each year. We also had a constant stream of pigs to slaughter, and extras to sell. Kidney stew was one of the results of this, and if you've never had it please don't torture yourself by trying it! There are some organs that should not be eaten—though in our house, you ate whatever was on your plate. Thank you, Mom, for drawing the line at tripe!

No one can forget the "black and yellow spiders". We would be merrily picking wild blackberries or raspberries and turn around and there was one right in front of your face! They were large and hung in their web in the middle of the day. They always hung around the berry bushes, presumably because that's where a lot of flies were to be found. I'm still afraid of spiders and have passed it on to some of my kids.

I used to like to go for long walks by myself. I probably would have liked someone to go with me but Christa and Ria were "bookworms" and never wanted to do anything. I had a favorite secret apple tree near the top of the dirt road. It had uniquely flavored wild apples and I didn't want anyone to know about it, maybe because it was not prolific. I used to climb up in it just to hang out, especially if I was mad about something. I've never had such apple perfection since. I looked for it on a recent trip to NY, but alas, it's gone.

I also liked going for walks in the winter. If there was a lot of snow, I'd use the snowshoes, but most of the time I just wore sneakers. Some years I might have had decent boots, but not always. I remember countless times having frozen feet. I explored every nook and cranny of our property (33 acres) and a lot of other people's property as well. Ria and I had a "fort" made of a few downed trees, and we gathered pieces of moss from the stream in the springtime and put them on the trees. Years later the moss was still growing into a beautiful patchwork of multi-colored greens. I always brought home wildflowers from my treks. I live in California now and every now and then I catch a whiff of some kind of flower that grew there and the memories flood in of hot summers on the farm.

One time, cousins Mary and Gail and I went trekking up behind the woods, thinking we would find the shortcut to West Winfield, and we cut through a plowed field. It was so muddy our feet sunk and it took forever to get through it. The mud stuck to our shoes and we plodded along carrying several extra pounds on our feet. We were gone for so long that people were starting to get worried.

Uncle Bunky was the Monopoly king. He would come for Thanks-giving or some other holiday and beat us thoroughly at Monopoly. No going easy on kids! He was a favorite though.

When Grandma and Grandpa came to visit from

Florida, they were the card sharks. Hearts was their game, and

I was usually too young to compete in any sense of the word. New Yorkers take their cards seriously! If a child can't compete, then don't play! I do not remember anyone wanting to take much time to teach me. You just had to figure it out by watching. I loved Pitch and also Black Jack when I was a bit older. We played cards and other games all winter long. When I was about 7, before the move, Terry taught me to do a bridge when shuffling the cards. I practiced until I perfected it and still impress people with it now. (It's easier than it looks.)

Some of us learned crafting skills during the long winters. Mom made mittens for everyone and a few of us also learned the trick of knitting them with 4 needles and no seams! No one knows where they all went, but mittens liked to sneak away when no one was looking. If you looked in the mitten drawer, you could easily find at least 20 unmatched mittens at any given time. Unless we were going to school, we'd just grab any 2 (or 4, depending on how cold it was!)

One year Dad decided it would be a good idea to take

me and the boys on individual fishing excursions, to spend time together. I cherish this memory, and at the time kept hoping for another turn. Dad took me to a small river, the Unadilla, and we took our tiny boat out in it to fish. It was a flat bottom aluminum boat with just enough room for 2, and had a tiny outboard motor and oars for backup. It was a warm, wet day after rain. I guess fish bite better at these times, at least that's what I was told.

I was a big wimp, and couldn't bear to put a worm on the hook—gross! Dad was probably disappointed in me, but he did it for me. I don't remember if we caught any (which probably means we didn't), but I do remember that he rowed out through a large patch of lily pads. I was wondering what he was up to, but soon found out. He was picking a water lily for Mom! What a romantic!

Dad was an early adopter and if he had lived long enough, he probably would have had one of the first generation iPods. He wasn't frivolous, buying unnecessary things, but he did keep up on important ones. I remember the first calculator he brought home. It was close to the size of a brick but thinner, with small red-lit numbers. What a great invention! It could only do the basic arithmetic. We couldn't use it for schoolwork though! He always liked taking pictures and we had a Polaroid camera. I remember it always seemed to be having trouble. When I look back at the pictures Dad took, a lot of them were blurry! Remember how you had to shake the photo and wait a few minutes for it to dry? Such a great invention. If you didn't like the picture you could take another without having to wait to get it developed. I'm sure

Dad would have had an early IBM clone in the 80's and a digital camera in the 90's.

Dad had been having heart trouble for a few years and we were all on the low salt diet. When he had his last heart attack, I remember he was sitting in the wagon wheel rocking chair by the wood stove in the dining room, either waiting for an ambulance to come or they were there taking his vitals. I was really scared and didn't know what to do or say. I could see he looked worried too. They took him to the hospital and I got to visit one time, but he was unconscious and on life support. He passed away a day or two later. I had the unwelcome duty of telling Paul, just because I came across him before anyone else did. It was a most difficult thing to do! I was 14 and Paul was 9. I smiled when I told him and he thought I was joking. Mom somehow carried on after that for four more years, patiently biding her time until I was out of high school.

What ever happened to the flag that the military gave Mom at Dad's funeral? Mike built a rock-bordered garden  around a tall flagpole and we flew it all the time. Unfortunately, whoever was in charge of bringing it in forgot, and there was a serious storm. It ripped it to shreds and tied it in a million knots (literally). I was probably the culprit but wouldn't admit it at that time.

I remember feeling so terrible that it happened, whether it was my fault or not.

This farm story ends shortly after my graduation with a marathon auction that went on far into the night, selling almost everything we owned. We had so much stuff that survived in the barn, they just kept pulling out more. I sold doughnuts and coffee and made a lot of money, but it went on so long I could have sold much more! Shortly after, I left for school in Boston and Mom, and "the boys" as they have always been collectively known, went with Mom and spent their remaining school years in a small suburban home near the gulf coast of Florida. I'm sure they felt the same as Terry, Mike and Susan did when they arrived at the farm! Ed was the same age as Terry had been.

One thing I am thankful for, no one had any serious illness or injury. Given how many of us there were, and all the animals and machinery, that's a miracle. Sure there were the usual childhood illnesses and a few car accidents, but nothing life threatening.

Our story is different from most farm experiences because of the brevity of it. 10 years, that's all it was. To me it was my whole childhood; I barely remember my life before the farm. But none of us could go home to the farm. It was gone, sold that day in the summer of '82 to someone else who couldn't possibly love it like we did. Who wouldn't take the same care of is as we did, who would change it! That was hard to grasp. Even though I was excited to be starting off as an "adult," I had no home to come home to. Christa was the only one who stayed in NY. Ria followed in Terry's footsteps, joining the Navy. Mike moved to Maryland and Susan had gone to Boston. (Eventually, almost all of us have served the armed forces, either as active duty or spouses.)

    Now, more than 30 years later, we are scattered across America, but our shared memories of the farm will always be with us and bond us together. We learned life skills on the farm that have served us well. We learned that no hurdle is too high and there's nothing we can't do once we decide to do it. We can buy an old antique and refinish it, or plant a garden in the city. If we want to learn to play an instrument, or knit a sweater, or learn to surf, or get a black belt, we just do it! We are always learning, and I think I can say that for every one of us. It's a no-limitations state of mind that we took from the farm.

98

Epilogue

I thought the new owners wouldn't love it as we did, but Ria's memories told me different:

"I've been back to visit the farm several times since Mom sold it. The last time was in 2007 before the owner who bought from us passed away. One of the trees in the front yard had been struck by lightning and he'd used the wood to make windowsills and the staircase! It was very nicely done. He had also completely gutted the upstairs and was dry walling new rooms, so that was something of a disappointment. I wanted to see what size my room was because it always seemed so huge when we lived there. I have Zada Livermore's little autograph book [from the 1800's found under the attic stairs, along with an old nailed boot.]"

There are new outbuildings and an addition to the barn. A garage juts out from the side of the house to where we once shoveled snow to our cars. (Why didn't we think of that?)

The pond has been filled in, some of the gardens turned back into pastures, the tiny fruit orchard has become mature and some have died out. And the old cemetery has been cleaned up and given the name East Street Cemetery and a historical plaque.

The home in 2004 with new garage addition

The home in the late 1800's with additional living space.

Made in the USA
San Bernardino, CA
03 September 2015